Black Country Dialectics

– a burlesque in poetry

Dave Wm Reeves

Black Country Dialectics

– a burlesque in poetry

✦

OFFA'S PRESS
2012

First published 2011 by Offa's Press
Ferndale, Pant, Oswestry, Shropshire, SY10 9QD
Second Edition 2012
ISBN: 978-0-9565518-3-2

Typeset in Baskerville Old Face

Designed by Début, Wolverhampton

Printed and bound by Steatham Colour Printers,
Wombourne, Staffordshire

CONTENTS

TRACKLIST

1. Saturday Night in Dodge City
2. A Black Country Guide to Computers
3. Trump That!
4. His Dark Materials
5. Stamp Shop
6. The Singularly Entertaining Ballad of Ayli Quixote and Sancho Aynuk etc.
7. (Fayt) Wuss Than Death
8. Bin (Owta circulation)
9. The Barrelfighter
10. Bionic Aynuk
11. The Harangues of the Cock Lectern of Wednesbury Parish Church
12. Toad Paradox
13. Springheel Jack's New Shoes

CD Produced by Chris Lomas

Black Country Dialectics
A burlesque in poetry

"What is termed humour in prose, I conceive, would be considered as burlesque in poetry"
William Shenstone – Essays on Men and Manners.

Acknowledgments: versions of some of these writings have previously been published as follows:
Boz in the Black Country was published in The Blackcountryman, Volume 10 issue 2, 1977; *A Black Country Fayre* as part of the broadsheet A Black Country Market, Dudley Poetry Centre 1980; *Ood a Thought it* and *Saturday Night in Dodge City* were published in *I scream Koans,* Stride Publications 1987; A Complete Banquet was published in *Thursdays* issue No. 9 October 1987; *From the Words of William Perry, The Tipon Slasher, Upon Finding His Quart Pot Empty* was published in the Black Country CAMRA Good Beer Guide, date not known.

This is as much the book of those I have met along the way, whose voices I have echoed: I dedicate it to them.

Ood a Thought it (Who'd have thought it)

Intro
There's possibilities in this life as you don't think about.
Speaking from personal experience, the more of them that you don't think about, the happier you are.
So there you are, happy and cheerful, going about your own business, when all of a sudden something happens, and all on account of somebody else's carelessness – or couldn'tcarelessness.
You don't know what to think of it, do you?
Do you!
Well I never do.
I wouldn't have thought that anybody could.
Well now, who'd have thought it, eh?

Incident I
We'd got hold of a reel of black cotton and with meticulous care we'd tied the one end to the railings and then wound it at least a thousand times between the railings and the lamp post on the other side of the pavement.
It was evening.
The beauty of black cotton is that in the twilight it can't be seen. Not at all.
We lurked. Down the pavement came Robby Crantree on his bike.
He rode straight into it. The shock unseated him.
"Yo shouldn't ride on the pavement," we shouted over our shoulders as we ran off – we ran straight into his mother.
"Y'young hoodlums".
"Hello Mrs Crantree".
"One of these fine days yo'm gonna really 'urt somebody doin' that, and then it'll be ood a thought it".
We hung our heads with shame.
"Be off with yer, an' don't yer let me see yer dooin' that agen, or by crikey there'll be 'Ell t'pay".
We ran off bravely laughing.
Robby cried as if it was 'one of these fine days' already, and he was the one who'd really been hurt.
We heard his mother's hand connect with the side of his head.
"I thought I'd towd yo' about ridin' on the paevement!"

Incident II
I'd got my finger up my nose.
Right up.
Second knuckle job.
I was reading at the time, not taking too much notice.
"One of these fine days, my lad, yo'll pull yer brains out doin' that –
and then it'll be ood a thought it!"

Outro
Ood a thought it?
Well, not me for one.
Not of him.
Anybody else, yes.
Not him though.
You can't credit it.
I used to sit by his mother at Sunday School.
Ood a thought it, eh -
Ood a thought it.

A Black Country Guide to Computers

'Computer jargon'

Wen I was a kidt
aardwier were buckits
were galvanised baths
besums 'n' brewems
'n' pairtent maastraps
ung fr'm the saylin
'n the paevement adawned

Warrisit now?
's a tayvay skrayn
wi' an owel in
t shuv in a disc

'N saftwier -
well, I spose
iss a claensuwt
aer a bikini in a
blizzerd

Bytes:
Beware o' the Stafford

Megabytes:
Beware o' the Rottweiler

Ram:
woolly thing -
wi' 'orns

Rom:
the rite rode a prnowncin
'ram'

Interfaece:
wat Daniel did in the lion's den
'Went interfaece the lions'

'Computer jargon'
an it duss
jars on the braen
like 15 pairnt o' mild.

A Cut Above

claerted fe' bein' born to a bally full o' beer
"the's no paece fer the wicked" they sed.

soo yer guessed tha's wat yo' must be - wicked
that ye'd never goo t'heaven

but the'r is a cut weer y'con drift wi'out haulin'
weer the's sun on the rushes an frittened coots squark

noo fites at the locks - noo lampins, noo urry
an yown gone theer now kid. they cor urt yer noo moor

Saftness

"On the whole, reading at home was regarded as a complete
waste of time. If anyone was seen with a book in their hands they
were soon told to go away and find something better to do."
from *'The Shambles, The Quack and Glory-for-me', reminiscences of
Blackheath & Rowley (1991).*

Saftness.
Why do' ya find summat useful t'do?
Yo'n allwys gotya yed inna book
It wo' get ya noweer.
Saftness.
The's steps t'be scrubbed
Yards t'be swept;
The cuttelrie's jew f'ra palish
It do stap y'knoe the 'ousewerk,
That wor Caxton's greyt invenshun
"the end've ousewerk as we knoe it,"
'Twor,
alluz 'e managed were ...
Saftness
Giz fowk ideas abuv th' staeshun
An meks ya goo blind
all that squintin':
meks my yed goo round juss watchin' ya:
Saftness
The's graetes t'be leaded
Fowds t'be swilled
but all yo'n got time for's -
Saftness.

The Singularly Entertaining Ballad of Ayli Quixote and Sancho Aynuk in which Ayli Quixote Mistakes the Pitheads of the Delph for Giants and Attacks Them.

This, the second part of our history, begins early one morning when the cobbled streets resounded with the clicking of steel-tipped sabots. Out from the Ummocks of the Gornals rode Don Ayli Quixote de la Gorsty Hill as he had styled hisself, taking the name of his place of domicile unto his own that he might honour it with his great doings, and his trusted page Sancho Aynuk.

On they rode in the misty morning past the Hall of Lord Russell toward the Hill near the Ley of Brier, where lived a dragon which belched flame and smoke, both in the daytime and in the nighttime. On they rode their nostrils ever flared by the reak of Bathams which wafted on the grit-thick air.
Then, below them, Quixote noticed giants whose dizzy heads rotated in a fashion most mocking.

"Aynuk", quoth the knight.
"Wass up?" came the firebrand reply.
"Dost see them theer giants?"
"Weer?"
"Theer".
"Weer?"
"Over theer."
"Weer's theer?"
"Theer!"

And thus we leave them and turn to verse.

Don Ayli Quixote, a moulder by trade,
Had been hit on the head by an ingot he'd made.
It knocked him down flat and addled his brain
Thus 'twas a knight errant that stood up again.

He went round next door where smoking his briar
Sat Sancho Aynuk, "Cum be mi squire",
To which Sancho agreed without further ado,
Owt t'get out o' the 'ouse an' 'e'd goo.

The pig sat on the wall to watch 'em goo by
He loffed soo much as he started to cry
"Wass up?" called the knight, not seeing the joke,
And with his halbert gid the pig a poke.

They rode cross the fields past owd Russell's Hall
And seeing Owd Russell they chanced him a call.
And down past the dragon that lived in Round Oak
And fetid the air with belched flame and smoke.

To where stood the giants, rigid and still,
Mocking our hero as he stood on the hill.
That wor t'be, no rowd at all
So he pulled out his sword and he answered the call.

He slashed at the fust un, or so I've heard tell,
But his skin was so tough that he shuddered like Hell,
With the force of vibration his armour came loose
And fell on the ground, "Stupid Owd Goose",

Said a ragged old tramp gleaning for slack,
"Yow'm gonna catch cowd wi' no clows on ya back!"

For there sat old Ayli, shocked and o'erwhelmed
His panoply down to long johns and his helm.

Thus did the knight errant find it neccessary to take the loan of
horse and cart onto which to load the remains of his armour. The
two of them then set forth in the direction of Netherton seeking
one Noah Hingley, a man purported to be wise in metals.

And in the next part of our history we shall learn of their journey,
how they fared, and how they picked up three old fridges, a bicycle
frame and a bag of old clothes on the way.

Unce, ther was grass

Unce
Afower ther was factories
Ther was grass

Then cum the advent o' the scythe
An' the need for sumweer t'mek it

Factories grew
An' grew
An' grew, spreadin' everyweer
As raysoned as Blind Mon's Buff,
Mekkin' moor an' moor,
Better an' better, scythes:
Until suddenly - ther was noweer t'use 'em

Unce
Afower ther was grass
Ther was factories.

A Black Country Fayre

i) Fair

Fair's fair, I always thought.
Down theer that do' mean nought
they'd tek the shirt off yer back.

They call 'em Wakes
now I see why
iss bloody early yo' must rise
wi' all the slayp
clayned from yer eyes
to pull one o'er on them.

Mountebanks on benches
winkin' at the wenches
as they palm coins an' eggs
sellin' o' their lotions
an' bottles full o' potions
fer arms an' chests an' legs.
But oh how it fills a hole in me
wen the fayrefolk cum t'town,
they goo, they leave the trodden green
I find the hole has grown.

ii) The Punch 'n' Judy Mon

I'd trust the mon
no further th'n
I cud pitch 'im down the strayt
ow con ya be
a friend of 'e
oos no moor th'n a booth wi fayt?

Cryin' in various voices
like the devil 'ad took 'is tongue
an playin' wi dolls like a little wench
an' toppin' it off wi' a song -
im as cor sing;
not a note.

Fayre folk. No moor t'be sed
it spakes fer itself
why I'd rather be jed
or tek as me friend a mischievous elf
than I'd down me a quart wi' the fayre folk.

iii) The Barrelfighter
Stondin' in a barrel
Blood all round me yed
In swam the bell o' the carousel
An' the baited bear was jed.
I sid the Maypole swayin',
I sid 'is faece spin past,
"Stond still ya sod, I'll get ya,"
But the world spun round too fast.
Me faece was busted open,
Me body stiff an' soor,
Wi' one moor punch 'e cud win the puss
An' the crowd cried out for moor.
We booth needed the money,
Yo' do' do this fer fun,
Soo I pulled meself t'gether
T'try fer a final run.
I 'it 'im an' 'e 'it me,

We gid an' took our all,
We arms felt limp, we muscles stapped,
An' t'gether we did fall.

The waeter cum as quite a shock
As they tipped the bucket up,
The world was blurred but I 'eared 'em say
"Our kid we wish yo' luck.
The puss is still a-stondin'
Cos neither on yer won,
Soo we've sed yo'll carry on our kid
An' sent word yo'll be late wum."

Boz in the Black Country

Recently I came across a collection of sketches and essays supposedly
from the pen of Charles Dickens, Esquire. After perusing them I
have no reason to believe these documents anything but genuine.
The following appears to have been a preliminary work for a novel,
for although it is in the first person there are hints of personal
history which are not consistent with that of the author.

"And so it was that I found myself at a party given by the Earl of
Dudley which was in the part attended by some of his servants and
their close relations.
One such fellow took it upon himself to approach me. He wore
moleskin breeches tied at the knee and a white scarf knotted
around his neck.

'Who'm yo'?'
'Pardon?'
'I sed, who'm yo' when yo'm at um?'

I assumed from his actually coming to me from the far side of the room that his intention was to become acquainted with myself.

'Wan ya do fo' a livin'?'
'I'm in iron.'
'Aye that a coincidence; soo's miself.'

We had apparently struck upon a mutual talking point.

'Wat part o' the bizness yo' in?'
'Construction. And yourself?'
'Tattin.'

''Ere, I say, I do' think much o' this perfumed waeter they'm a gi'in we, dun yo'?'
'It's Moselle. A German wine.'
'I'd much rather 'ave a pint o' Bathams.'
'I beg your pardon?'
'I sed, I'd much rather 'ave a pint o' Bathams.'

I must at this point admit my ignorance and say that I had never heard of 'Bathams', but after an explanation of its ambrosian qualities by my newfound companion I found myself sorely desiring to partake of the beverage.

Thus we went, my companion and myself, to an alehouse which stood in the vicinity and partook of the said 'Bathams'.
Truly it was an ale of the finest taste, clarity and, though I only began to realise this on reflection, strength.

'Wan ya think on it then mi mon?'
''T's goat in nexceptional.....mmmm....about it.'

18

'Berra than that stuff we was drinkin' afower wat?'

But, and I admit this with more than a modicum of shame being
something of a porter drinker, I found myself somewhat indisposed,
prostrate, and covered in sawdust.'"

Bin (Owta Circulation)

Weer'n ya bin?

Loony, thas weer I'n bin
the fer side-elseweer
weer it grows on yer parms
on the full mooan 'v evry day
weer we do spake on
                case i's catchin'
weer's fowk as cor cope
        an we an too, do' we: no option but
weer's desertion to be shot fer
                    wen y'ger um

too much time f'reflection
      if yo' keep lookin' in that mirrer
      yo'll see the devil o'er yer showder
      owd Nick, as finds werk fer idle onds
bes' kayp busy
aer i's baskets fer thee onds
           that aer mailsacks.

Saturday Night in Dodge City

(In the 19th Century a great number of people from the industrial Black Country emigrated to America to escape poverty. With them they took their dialect and their culture. Now read on ....)

i)
"Oi yo' I'm callin' yo' out!"

Saturday night in Dodge City
And Billy the Kid is angry.

"A pint o' mild an' a bag o' scratchin's luv."

One foaming jug whizzing along the polished bartop.
One foaming jug stopped by the hand of Billy the Kid.
He sucks the froth between the remnants of his teeth
And waits

And waits

And waits

"Weer's mi scratchin's?"
"Ain't got no scratchin's."
"Wanya mean, no scratchin's?"
"We ain't seen Jabez fer weeks."

ii)
Out in the wilderness Jabez Taylor, Doctor (selfstyled),
whistled as he wielded a spluttering skillet over an open fire.

"'Urry up with them strips o' skin wench, the pon's 'ot."

"Warris it, anyrode up. I cor cut it. It surely t'God aye pig!"
"Cudn't get no pig, it's buffalo. They woe know the difference."

'Dr Jabez Taylor's Medicine Show and Scratchin' Waggon'
read the sign on the side of the covered wagon.
"Come you people gather round,
Jabez Taylor's back in town."

"In this bottle what I'm holdin' 'ere is Doctor Jabez Taylor's
Wonder Potion, guaranteed, without argument, to cure the human
body of coughs, colds, piles and to bring back childlike smiles to
the depressed and woebegotten. Containing over one hundred
different herbs."

iii)
"I'n eared it towd
As around I've rode
Across these plains and prairies
From them as've cum
From the plaece as wus um
To me parents, me uncles 'n' aunties
As Jabez Taylor 'ad t'flee
From the Tip'n Wakes one year
An' tek the fust boat 'cross the sea"
Sed Billy the Kid to his beer.

iv)
"Tay wuth the trouble" - said Billy the Kid, drinking alone at the bar.
"Tay wuth frettin' over: no scratchin's.
Giz another mild."

The joanna jingled in the corner.

"Gorr any crisps?"
"Nope. Sir Walter Raleigh pinched all the 'tatas."
"Giz another mild."

Doc Holiday dealt another hand of crib.

"It ain't as if I really want any,
iss onny force of 'abit."
He drummed his fingers on the bar.
"Giz another mild."

"OH DAMN IT!"
I'm off to find me that Jabez Taylor
an' when I findin' 'im there aye nothin'
as I ain't gonna do to 'im."

But just then
the swing doors swung
and through them strode a hawker.

v)
"Cockles
Mussels
Whelks."

The folk could hardly believe their eyes
'Twas Jabez Taylor in another guise.

"Oi yo', I'm callin' yo' out!"

From the Words of William Perry, The Tipton Slasher, Upon Finding His Quart Pot Empty

The fust un to bellock I'll bost!
I turned me back, I turned back round, me quart of ale's now gone
And me pot stonds mutely on the bar, iss grievin' me.
Yet I know damn well that much um brew, when guzzled down in one,
Wull rise back up the wazzin an' struggle to be free.
Soo the fust un to bellock I'll bost!

Portrait

Send the kids down the pub
T'see if there's any money left.

Thee dinner's in th' oven
dried out bi now.

I'm sick of it
wik after wik.

A Complete Banquet

Pt 1: hors d'oeuvre

"Mr Kevin Woodford, head of catering technology at Granville College, is taking 20 students and four staff to prepare a banquet for 60 at Chamalieres, Clermont Ferrand. Mr Giscard d'Estaing, former president of France, may be among the guests.
The French, Mr Woodford said, would eat "good British commodities, wholesomely cooked but presented in the modern fashion." It would be "the type of thing your grandmother would have cooked.""

The meal consists of:

"....... a tartlet filled with chopped field mushrooms topped with a lightly poached quail's egg, accompanied by a tartlet case made of smoked salmon, filled with smoked salmon mousse. From there, the French will continue with Chatsworth game terrine, a mosaic of rabbit, hare and venison set in a jelly of port wine and green peppers.
The fish course is a casserole of Manx queenies (baby scallops) with creamed spinach dumplings, followed by a sorbet of Scotch whisky and pink grapefruit.
As a main course, the students will present heart of loin of English lamb with a sort of skinless sausage of spring vegetables and new potatoes, all set in an essence of port wine, lemon mint and honey. Different English goat cheeses on hot sultana bread, will be followed by "a trilogy of chocolate puddings" each laced with a different liqueur, Bronte liqueur, Drambuie and Tia Maria. Sweetmeats complete the banquet."

from The Guardian Monday 23/3/87

Pt 2: entree

it was a long time agoo an' i do' quite remember what me granny used t'cook, or 'ow 'er used t'cook it, but i do remember the look on me granfaether's faece when 'e looked at 'is dinner

"goo on chap an' tek this t'yer granfaether," me granny'd say
handin' me the white puddin' basin with a cloth over the top of it,
tied up with a piece of string which looped up to form a handle

an' off i'd goo down the road at a pace cos i could 'ear the
factory bull roarin' in the distance an' i knew they'd be out at
any minute an' starvin' f'ther vittels, swingin' the basin as little as poss

granfaether's face was black from the foundrydust, eyes
sparkled as 'e sid me appraoch, shoutin' a lot cos the ommerin'
never stopped in 'is 'ead, loads of other kids runnin' wi' covered basins

"wot we got t'day?" 'e'd say, peelin' back the cloth
an' peekin'. 'e'd gi' me a piece o' bread dunked in the liquor,
i eat it slow while i waited for the basin; it was lovely:

to my palate, to granfaether's palate, it was manna
sustenance, a little bit of love in the middle of a hard
day in the middle of a hard life. To us it was

a tartlet filled with chopped field mushrooms topped with a lightly
poached quail's egg, accompanied by a tartlet case made of smoked
salmon, filled with smoked trout mousse.
It was Chatsworth game terrine, a mosaic of rabbit, hare and venison
set in a jelly of port wine and green peppers.
It was a casserole of Manx queenies (baby scallops) with creamed
spinach dumplings, followed by a sorbet of Scotch whisky and pink
grapefruit.
It was heart of loin of English lamb with a sort of skinless sausage of
spring vegetables and new potatoes, all set in an essence of port wine,
lemon mint and honey. It was different goat cheeses on hot sultana
bread. It was a "trilogy of chocolate puddings" each laced with a
different liqueur.
It was coffee and sweetmeats. A complete banquet.

Pidgin English

Loft .....
   I'll say
Loft .....
   I cooda criad
sat theer wi a clock
as cudn't be stapped
watchin the claeds
goo by.

Ummin?
   The's no plaece
like it, but this'n cudn't
ayven 'um the chewn

Alluz I whant
is a ring t'stap tyme
alchemy wi wings as's
stapped aff ooer the brine
fun sum branch a
Ararat t'drap iss
deposit on

Fayt at full tilt
from loft t'Layjun
'Arken:
jossle on paevement

dooerjam 'n' claem

Tew dark t'see now
the specs cum in,
see'm circle 'n' coo

dinner's cood on the taeble
aspiraeshuns 'awkd
Fantaels spreddin lung the
Layjun bar.

Winter in Wartime

Cooed:
Chrysanths unched
agin wintas
breathfast twinkle
the mouthclaed
'n smuther t'cum
Waetin':
we'n gorra goo on
b'yoe cor f'ge' the telergram
as might cum threw
th'dooer
Chill:
A glashya's ponda'd crayp
The arbitrie suck
o' farewell.

Toad Paradox

When I was a child I was always
bein' tode t'be tode:
'Yo' be tode,' I was tode. Yet
I knew damn' well that if I went an' sat
squat on me 'aunches, goggle-eyed an' gulpin',
aer chose 'oppin as a mode of ambulation
I'd get a cuff round th'earhole

An by cuff I doe mean a germ laden
spasm o'the bronchial tract powered
bi an involuntary squaygin' o' the lungs.
Tay wor I mean. Tay.
An while that itself, tay, might also suffice
fer the word fer a brewed beverage o'
dried leaves,
besides bein' the word fer the light meal
that comes either before or after yer dinner,
dependent (an' if yo' aft' ask 'dependent on what'
yo' certainly aye got any concept
of the British caste system, as I con see)
I'm simply usin' it here as the negative. Tay.
Tay war I mayn at all.

But to get back to the paradox …
Was I tode? Did I become the sort of person
Yo' could rub on a wart 'n' it'd drap off?
Did the insistence that 'That'll learn yer'
actually achieve its objective: Was I taut?
Wound tight, my friends: wound tight
an' ready to snap.

Vile Ada

Do I know vile Ada?
Yow know vile Ada.
Do I know vile Ada?
Vile Ada: yow know.

I dow remember.
Yow knew 'er mother.
I dow remember.
Yow knew 'er brother.
I dow remember.
Yow knew 'er sister,
Yow remember.
But I dae know 'er.

Ar,
I knew 'er mother,
I knew 'er brother,
I knew 'er sister,
But I dae know 'er.

Dae ya know vile Ada?
No, I dae know Ada.
I thought yow'd know vile Ada.
No, I dae know 'er.
But yow knew 'er sister?
Oh, I knew 'er sister.
Well I'm talkin' 'bout 'er sister,
'Ave yow 'eard ....?

Stamp Shop

I got them in pocketfuls, sat there amazed on days
when the sun shone and I should have been outside

Squares, rectangles, faces, heads, animals, aeroplanes,
buildings, bridges, plants, flags, ships, unnameable fruits

A ruckus of travellers
retired, be-albumed, flat between pages
like the crushed spirit of a flower,
And pondered

on journeys to
Greece and Uganda,
Rhodesia and Spain,
Cuba, Argentina,
Russia: places that
the red buses never rolled their
canvas destination, never ran

I wanted to work in a stamp shop
could think of no better way
to live as an adult

*

Well I work in a stampshop now
And the hammers pound down
Knocking out heavier shapes

There's thuds in the morning
Like western front guns

The ground shakes, and yer boones shake with it
It knocks the air from yer lungs
Rattles the teeth in yer yed

Your brain cells get drummed
Thoughts tekkin' flight, confused and impoverished refugees
Fighting to keep some semblance of reason
Some suitcase of geegaws
Some photo of what was
Some sandbagging against the war
A philosophy to hang onto
when you are feeling hung out to dry
A sheet to slip out the back window
when the Press comes bullmouthed to drag you from your bed
                and sign you up for the shilling
An ideology, an old time religion
for when you try to go your own way and get confused in the
inarticulateness of your educating

When you start to debate with the PhD of your soused knuckles
Giving a Jolly Rogering to them as talk the company line
In the
Yo ho ho and a battle of rum ideas

It's me
        had the corners crimped
been bought: stuck

Has dropped into the dark after the last collection.

(Fayt) Wuss than Death

Faetha kept a belt behind the kitchen door
And if e took that belt down you could be sure
Someone was gonna get a lampin'
       bright enough to light their way
to
a reviewing of their attitude
a reassessment of their situation
a seeing of the wrong of their ways

but it never came down as I remember
just hung on its peg a reminder
of what could be
of what might happen:
      a Christ on the cross
      a head on a stake
      a slave displayed along the Via Appia
      a Doom in a Medieval church
      a stiff in a gibbet
           blowing in the wind
and whatever Hell was in that leather
was no compare to the measure
of awe in which we held faetha's pedal extremities
because when he took his boots off
you was in for fayt wuss than death

When 'e sat bi the fire with 'is fayt on the 'ob
'twas amazin' 'ow we cud all find a job
needed doin out in the yard
no matter the weather, the rain, wet and cooed
tropical heatwave ayr blizzard that blooed

No weather cud soften our ardour
owt was better than sittin' wi' faetha
getting' impaled on the spikes of stale sweat
that rose from is boots and is fayt: wuss than death.

Kismet?
Yo' wudn't kiss is fayt I'll tell yer
No toesuckin in the boudoir of our back-to-back

just a paediatrician's nightmare
rearing up on its hind legs and pawing at the air
as if it wanted to get out of the room as well –
perhaps that's why faetha slept s'good

The goblins and the gremlins
kept at bay by the odour that issued
forth, fifth and sixth from his 'obnails
The ghouls and twisted fiends
sent from the dark side of repose
(or an ill advised cheese and pickle sandwich last thing)
forced gagging into the corner of the bedroom with the commode
unable to advance the *grand jeté* of their demonic dance
into the dreamscapes of the slumberer
for fear of faetha's fayt: wuss than death
an' they should know.

'Ow mutha stood it I've no idea, but one should ne'er surmise
about other folk's relationships, and they say there's none soo blind
as them in love – though I've never eared anything said
about it affecting the sense of smell

it was as if the day they got together 'er clocked off
at the olfactory and never clocked back on again

for richer or for poorer, in sickness or in health
stond by yer mon, however bad 'e smells

But that belt ...
Remember the belt? The one on the back of the door.
I often wonder what became of it.

Whilst Arranging Flowers at the Graveside

I dreamt of yo' last night.
Theer yo' was stondin afower me;
young wench wrapped in a shawl,
fragile, surrounded by smoke,
light be'ind yer (like a ghost) -
comin' out of a foundry
all flaeme an' impenetrable cloud
like the fust time I sid yer
just stondin', lookin', waitin'
we 'ad to wait then wench -
cum coortin' an yer muther'd
gi me bread an' drippin' fer supper
twas wuth the waitin' to be together.
Just stondin' yer was
I wanted yer to reach yer hand out ....
Then the bull went fer the end of the shift:
7 o'clock an' the alarm was gooin'.
It wo' be long wench
It wo' be long.
God bless.

Tell me some pitying Angel
(after Purcell)

Weer's 'e gone? I doe know
yoe cor turn yer back fer a minnit
As if yoe aye gor'enuff t'werrit abaet
wi'out 'avin' 'im gooin' missin
Yoe need eyes in the back of yer yed wi that one
An iss no good sayin' "I'll tell yer faether"
cos all 'e sez iss "'E already knows
an' con yoe see forty days wuth o' nimbostratus?
con yoe see a plague o' frogs?
con yoe see temples doin' the tumble o' displeasure?
am I turned into a pillar o' salt?"
"No" I'll say "but at least yo'd be of sum value if yoe was"
An then I regret it - as yoe dun
Yoe cud bite yer tongue off sumtimes. Kids.
Get out fromn under me feet yoe'll say
Goo 'n' play in the sawdust or summat
An then, as soon as yoe realize yoe aye sid 'em fer an hour...

NOTES

Aynuk & Ayli are the Everyman characters of Black Country folklore and humour. They are the naïves, the simple folk who we identify with and who allow us to laugh at ourselves. They are akin to the Paddy & Mick of Irish humour and as comedian Billy Russell said, in his introduction to the 1968 Black Country Stories published by the Black Country Society: 'During the Industrial Revolution, many 'sons of Erin' came to the Black Country to put their muscle into the heavy industries ... I often wonder did they bring something else with them beside their brawn? I have found that nowehere in Great Britain is there a greater similarity of the humour of the Irish and that of the Black Country'.

The Tipton Slasher was prizefighter William Perry, all England bare knuckle boxing champion 1850-1857. Born in Tipton, he is buried in Kates Hill Cemetery, Dudley.

Bellock.: to belch. The wazzin: the gullet.

The Cut. Still used as the word for canal in the Black Country. The 'cut' was the word that the navigators would have used for the channel they were digging through the earth, the cut through the ground that would later be filled with water.

Barrelfighting. Strap two empty barrels together. Stand bareknuckle boxer in each. Commence fight.

Boz in the Black Country was first published in The Blackcountryman and resulted in a visit from the local press to interview the author of the piece. Not because of its literary merit but because the editor had noticed that the centenary of the opening of Batham's brewery was then being celebrated meaning that it was not opened until 7 years after Dickens' death.

Whilst Arranging Flowers at the Graveside was written during an Arts Council residential week at Ty Newydd, Criccieth in November 1996. Something of the melancholy of working in the room where David Lloyd George died seems to have stirred up the hiraeth.

In many of these pieces there is a mix of Black Country dialect and what, for want of another description, we will call Standard English. The simple fact is that while I was born into a community that communicated in dialect, as I grew older much of the old language died and was replaced with a hybrid. Here I have heard voices from different times of my life as I have written the poems, and have transcribed them. There are also times when people from the area speaking in Standard English, myself included, will inadvertently drop in a dialect word or phrase. This is an attempt to represent the voices I hear, explore the arguments my language has with itself, not write in the vernacular purely for comic effect.